TRANSFORMATION BY DESIGN

Transform Your Life
One Challenge at a Time

CoachTY

10-10-10
Publishing

Transformation By Design
www.coachty.ca

Copyright © 2020 CoachTY

ISBN: 978-1-77277-353-8

Publisher
10-10-10 Publishing
Markham, ON   Canada

Printed in Canada and the United States of America

Table of Contents

I am dedicating this book to my grandparents, Maisy and Chesterfield Gill, the pioneers and foundation of our family.

My parents, Norma Estelle and Herbert A. Hinds:
Mom, for your unconditional love, humble nature and for always being there for me; Dad, for your determination and hard work.

My sister, Marva, aka Pat, for your kind heart and generous nature. It's hard to believe you are gone, but I give thanks for having the opportunity to experience the love you shared with me.
Rest in peace.

My siblings—Margaret, Beverley, and Junior and their families, thank you all for being there for me and supporting me.

Special blessings to my children, Tyrone Jamien, Tyler Malone, and Joy Victoria Hinds;
to my grandchildren, Aryana, Jamien, and Josiah Hinds
and to any future grandchildren.
Love you all.

Acknowledgements

I would like to start by giving thanks to the Creator, for life and for being able to share my story.

Thank you to my family and friends. Thanks to Nancy Jamieson for all her support and generosity, and for being my biggest cheerleader and partner.

To my friends and family in Montreal, the UMOJA community, and to my conscious brothers— Jamal, Dalton, Sando, Jamie, Karl, Keith, Marcus, Phillip and Amassey.

All of my Montreal, CDN people who have helped in my growth. The people I grew up with, played ball with, and partied with.....you know who you are.

To my loyal clients and founding members—Mary-Jo, Sharon, Bonnie, Ginny, Nancy, Dal, Mary-Ann, Sue, Robin, Wendy, David, Louise, Miro, Jan, Gabor, and Nick—and to all the people I have worked with and trained over the years.

A special big "up" to Doctor Michael K. Jones, the creator and president of the Medical Exercise Specialist program. This program was a life changer for me and a must-do program for every personal trainer, therapist, or anyone looking for ways to bridge the gap between health care and fitness.

Thank you to Doctor Earl Bogoch and his team for helping me walk pain-free again.

A special thanks to Raymond Aaron for creating the 10-10-10 program. It was just what I needed to accomplish my goal of writing a book.

Some other motivators and mentors: Harry Lorayne, author of *The Secrets of Mind Power*, which was the first book I read on my journey to personal development; and Anthony Robbins, Jim Rohn, Bob Proctor, Joe Vitale, Mind Valley Academy, Brian Tracy, Lisa Nichols, John Assaraf and many more I have come across in my life time.

Foreword

How are you aging? Are you energetic, enthusiastic, and purposefully living? Are you vibrating at your highest frequency? If not, then *Transformation By Design,* by Coach Ty is a must-read.

Coach Ty's knowledge and expertise, combined with his own personal story of overcoming meningitis and bilateral hip replacement, will affect the way you approach each and every day.
His passion to discover alternative therapies, coupled with his experience and knowledge of the human body, makes Coach Ty a highly sought after authority.

The techniques used in his own recovery process, combined with years of studying the Laws of the Universe and working in the fitness industry, all come together in this powerful book.

Coach Ty will help you increase your vibrational level and transform yourself. As an active ager, I happily suggest you read and adopt Coach Ty's philosophies.

Be the best version of you and live life to its fullest.

Raymond Aaron
New York Times Bestselling Author

Chapter 1

My Story

I'm an old-school boomer, and like every person, I have a story. My family and I immigrated from Barbados W.I to Montreal when I was about three years of age. We stayed with my grandparents for the first few years. During that time, I acquired some of the skills and the mindset that would help me make it through the challenges I encountered in later years.

The first things I learned were discipline and hard work. My grandparents showed me these skills through their efforts and tenacity. These skills allowed them to bring our whole family to Canada. When I think back about that experience, it baffles my mind. How could two people leave a small island and come across the ocean to another world, a place where they had to overcome many challenges just to survive, let alone save enough money to bring our whole family to Canada?

My grandparents were pioneers and true heroes for our family, and for many more families that came later.

When we arrived in Montreal, we stayed downtown in an area called Little Burgundy. My three sisters attended school, and I stayed home with my mother. My father was studying to be an electrician and would take jobs wherever he could find them. My dad taught me that hard work and the willingness to work pays off.

After a few years, my parents decided to move and get their own place.

Our first family apartment was in Cote-des-Neiges, on Barclay Street. This is where I went to elementary and high school, and continued to learn valuable lessons.

When I was 5 years old, my dad had my sisters and I walk from our home to our grandparents' home, which was approximately 5 miles away. My dad's insistence on walking made me stronger and more determined when I started school and playing sports.

That walk was the beginning of old school training for me. Imagine a man walking faster than the average person. Now, imagine a 5-year-old trying to keep up with that man. That walk taught me to try my best, not complain, and be determined.

"The walk" turned me into a strong competitor that made me give my all every time I competed. I had an extraordinary amount of energy. Being one of the smallest students in school, I always had to push a little harder to be competitive in sports and the games we played. All of these things gave me more heart and helped me to see my competitor in a different light. As time went on, I got better at dealing with all types of challenges.

In gym class, we did a lot of gymnastics—things like climbing the big rope that hung from the ceiling, about 20 plus feet high.

We also did the rings and the horse, as well as the spring board, which was one of my favourites. The gym teacher, Mr. Schillack, would always call on me to demonstrate how to do a particular exercise, mainly because I was athletic, competitive and small. This gave me more confidence in my abilities, which would be useful in later years.

High School

When I started high school, things were quite different from elementary school. When it came to sports, all of the activities and sports I had played in elementary school were no longer part of the agenda. The sports that we were introduced to consisted of soccer, volleyball, football, and basketball.

I personally love playing football, but I did not like having to wear all of that equipment, as it felt too restrictive to me. I tried out for soccer as I had the skills and the quickness necessary. I did not like playing outside when it was snowing, when all we had on was shorts and a T-shirt. The next logical sport for me to play was basketball. Being 5 feet tall, I was not the ideal size for the sport; however, because of my competitiveness and my abilities, I decided to give it a try. My jumping and my ball handling skills were above average. I recall watching the senior team playing, seeing some of them touching the rim, and others dunking, which was amazing to me.

I wanted to touch the rim, but I could barely touch the net. Touching the rim became my first goal. My determination and constant practice helped me improve every day.

After many attempts, and probably a month later, I finally touched the bottom of the net. The feeling was awesome, and I wanted to get better and jump higher.

Back then, I was already setting goals. At that time, I had no knowledge about goal setting or anything like that. I just wanted to touch the rim and, maybe someday, dunk the ball. I kept on visualizing and practicing until it was manifested.

The skills mentioned above are skills we all tried to learn as kids. We had great imaginations; we visualized ourselves doing things before we could do them.

Fast forward a few months, and I'm focused and determined to touch the 10-foot basketball rim. At this time, I was about 6–8 inches away from the rim. When your mind and body work together, anything can happen. The day finally came when I touched the rim. That was a celebration for me on so many levels. That accomplishment gave me the confidence to go even further.

By the end of the year, I was jumping and touching the rim at will.

My jumping ability was so good that I could stand under the rim and jump vertically and grab it with both hands. This was a big deal for someone just over 5 feet tall.

I had other passions, like dancing and music. We had a small group of guys that would go to the music room at lunch time so that we could play percussion instruments. We didn't have much music training, but every one of us loved making music—beating the drums, and playing the xylophone or anything we could that made a cool sound.

Our small group would play whenever we had a chance. When we weren't playing, we would be in the gym shooting hoops. I loved basketball so much that I played every day, and once or twice a week the gym would be open at night and we would play some pick-up ball. This was at our high school, North Mount High.

On the off nights, when our gym was closed, we would go to Logan High School to play ball. Logan High was about a mile and a half away from the apartment. My best friend Dalton and I would walk up to Logan to play some pick-up ball. We did this during the school season. During the summer holidays we would play at Bedford high school, on the out door court.

Back in the day, we would walk home in subzero weather with running shoes and a thin jacket, just to look hip. When we got home, our hands and feet would be frozen.

A few times, I couldn't use my keys because my hands were so stiff. No matter how bad it was, we continued to go and play ball.

We had the tenacity and ambition to play basketball and improve our skills. In my early years, I focused on basketball and dancing. I loved to dance, and I was pretty good at it.

In high school, Gary, Ralph and I (Tyrone) decided to enter the talent show.

I believe it was Gary who came to Ralph and me, and suggested we audition for the variety show.

When we knew we would be in the show, we would rehearse every day after school. We practised for weeks. All of the practice paid off, because we got pretty good.

The night of the show, I was anxious, but I knew we had our routine down to the T. We took things a step further and went out and purchased matching black corduroy suits.

We purchased some star studs and placed them down the side of our pants and on the arms of the jackets. Each of us put the first letter of our name on the back. We became T.R.G., which was Tyrone, Ralph, and Gary.

Our first dance was to "Funky President," by James Brown. The crowd went wild in a standing- room-only auditorium. I felt anxious when I peeked out before the show and saw how big the crowd was but after hearing the applause and receiving a standing ovation, all my anxiety vanished. I felt awesome and was ready for the next dance routine.

Our next dance routine was to the song Machine Gun by the Commodores. Our routine was spot on, and the crowd went crazier than they had with the first song. After that performance, things changed and we became famous in our hood and school.

My first job after high school was working for McDonald's as a morning cook. This experience gave me skills that I continue to use today: responsibility, punctuality, and discipline. I was still interested in continuing my education, but my main goal at that time was to get my driver's license.

Working at McDonald's allowed me to reach my goal. I worked there for about a year.

After McDonald's, I worked in a factory doing a very boring job.

The job was separating a roll of material into a stack or pile—that was it. I struggled to keep my sanity, and counted every minute of the day. I worked there for about 6 months.

After that job, I decided I needed something more. I found out about a program in Toronto where I could improve my skills and be better prepared for life. It was my best friend, Dalton, that told me about the program and he was going to take it. The school was DeVry Institute of Technology. I took the electronic technician course, and Dalton took the technology course. I always wanted to get into broadcasting, and that program looked like the way to go.

After a year of school, money got tight and I had to stop and work full time. That turned out to be a blessing. I applied for a job as a fitter/assembler with a small company. The pay was good, and the company had eight employees. They took me under their wing and enrolled me in a certified program to become a fitter assembler.

During my time working at the company, I got my first opportunity to see Canada from coast to coast. I always wanted to travel and see all of Canada. I got the opportunity to do that, as well as travel to Europe for a month, where I visited Germany, France, and Switzerland. That was one of the highlights in my life at that time, and the realization that I could manifest the things I wanted in my life. I have always been a big believer in education and the laws of attraction and manifestation, as well as directing and controlling energy.

The company shut down around Christmas that year, and I was unemployed for a while. I ended up going back to school. This time, I went to George Brown College.

I took a program called E.O.S., which stood for electronic office systems. In this course, we learned how to repair computers and electronic devices.

I already had the foundations of electronics, so the course was easy for me. This gave me some extra time to get involved in student clubs and programs. The school had a radio station that was looking for broadcasters. I auditioned, and I received a 2-hour spot a couple of times per week. This was a dream come true for me.

Volunteering at the college radio station was a great opportunity for me to learn the workings of a radio station. My overall time at George Brown College was rewarding, both educationally and socially. I started playing table tennis and became quite proficient at it.

I also continued playing basketball, and did weight training at the gym. When I wasn't at school, I was looking for opportunities to make money. I had this thing for promotions and putting events together. I would do a few disc jockey gigs on weekends, and I also started selling an assortment of products at a flea market spot I rented.

My mind was mainly focused on business and promotional opportunities, so I was always attracting interesting ventures and Ideas.

The extra money helped me subsidize the limited amount of money I was getting from the government sponsored program.

Everything worked out well for me. It gave me the opportunity to go to school and get money to live and pay my bills.

When I finished my schooling, my first job was working as a photocopier technician, repairing and refurbishing Canon copiers in the shop.

After 6 months, I got promoted to a field technician, where I would do repairs in customers' locations. I enjoyed dealing with the customers face to face, and I gave excellent customer service. This allowed me to become a sales rep.

I enjoyed sales and the psychology of the interaction with customers. This love for sales, and the opportunity to learn about people, intrigued me. I still have the love for learning and interacting with others.

The sales game was and still is part of my life. With many years in the field and working in all types of sales positions such as retail, door-to-door, business cold calling, telemarketing etc. I have sold everything from shoes, clothing, cars, electronic office equipment, insurance, fitness memberships, etc.

After numerous positions and educating myself on result-oriented sale techniques, I came across a company that would give me the opportunity to use my sales techniques to become a district manager, and eventually have my own business.

I started working for Dickie Dee Ice Cream as a sales supervisor, and after my first season, I was promoted to district manager. I believe Dickie Dee was the best company I had worked for. I learned many useful skills and had a remarkable customer retention rate of 92%, which involved keeping my distributors happy, and assisting them when they had needs. The following year, I decided to take on a distributorship myself.

I worked out a deal where I could run the business and still work as a district manager. Everyone was happy. During that year, many records were broken, and lots of product was sold. Dickie Dee gave me a good foundation for business and customer service.

After an eight-year relationship with Dickie Dee Ice Cream, the company was sold to Unilever. The sale of Dickie Dee was unexpected, and my position as district manager came to an end a year later. When this happened, I decided to sell my distributorship and move to the USA.

Chapter 2

Life Changing Events

Moving to the USA was a life changing event for me. I had just sold my ice cream business, and I wanted to make some changes in my life. I decided to move to Rochester, NY. My dad had been living there for many years.

Two of my sisters had also moved there a couple of years prior to my decision to move. I decided to use my green card, I thought Rochester would be the best place to start the next chapter of my life, especially if I wanted to live in the States.

At that time, I had some money and the connections to get a custom-built dream home. I thought I had worked things out so that by the time I moved, everything would be ready. Things, however, didn't work out as planned, and I ended up staying at my sister's place for 3 months.

After a few months of waiting for my house to be completed, I had a severe Achilles tendon rupture. I got injured playing basketball at the local YMCA in Rochester. This injury laid me up for about 6 weeks. At that time, I didn't want to have an operation, so the doctor placed my lower leg in a cast.

When I look back on that situation, I wish I had had the operation. Most people that had the operation were up and back to themselves in a few months.

My healing took a lot longer. The tenderness lasted for a few years. The whole experience limited my vertical jumping ability by a few inches, although I could still touch the basketball rim.

My time in Rochester was definitely a challenge, to say the least. I went through many ups and downs. The struggles and the stresses of keeping my home and keeping my relationship together were difficult. My spouse didn't have her papers to live in the USA, so she decided to go back to her parent's home, in Brantford, Ontario, Canada. This was a hard transition for me, because I would go back and forth two times per week, and sometimes on the weekends as well.

The stress of the driving, crossing the border, and managing my situation took a toll on me.

After a year and a half of constant back and forth driving from Rochester to Brantford, combined with not taking good care of myself, my health started to deteriorate. I was renting my home out, living at my father's place, and trying to keep things together. With everything that I was going through, my stress level climbed, and unfortunately, I got ill.

I didn't know what was happening to me. All I remember is being at work and feeling very sick to my stomach. A short time later, I had to leave and go home.

When I arrived home, all I could do was lie down. When I tried to eat, I threw everything up. I thought I had the flu and I believed my body was telling me to take it easy. I didn't listen, and eventually it made me listen.

My diet was bad, I was eating frozen microwave dinners from Walmart. The next time you have a chance, look at the label to see the sodium amount in those dinners. The numbers are out of this world.

On top of all the stress and the bad diet, I remember having a mosquito bite on my upper arm, just below my deltoid muscle. The itching went on for at least 3 months, and a small bump remained. I didn't pay much attention to the fact that it persisted, because the itching was intermittent, and I was so busy dealing with other issues. I believe the mosquito transferred meningitis to me. Everything started to come together as I looked back on all the events. I recalled, in my early childhood, the event that probably started everything.

How the Meningitis Was Started

I believe it was when I was in grade one or two. I remember there was a park on the other side of the fence from the school. Every recess, all the children would run around the fence or climb it to play. I was one of the climbers. I had accomplished this task many times, but this particular day, my regular climb and jump didn't work out as expected. I climbed the fence as usual, but when I went to jump down, my shoe lace got caught on the top of the fence, and I fell down, right on the top of my head. I believe I had a concussion. When I stood up, I was dizzy, and my head and neck hurt quite a bit. I never told anyone, mainly because I was embarrassed by my actions, and I thought my mom would be angry with me. I did the unthinkable and kept it to myself.

The stiff neck and pain lasted for a couple of weeks. I thought I was good, so I never gave it much thought. I did experience occasional dizzy spells and a sensation of not knowing where I was. The sensation felt like the feeling you get when you are dehydrated. I didn't like that feeling, but it only came on me every few months.

The sensation and dizzy spells continued for years but would be farther apart each time. By the time I was in my early 20s, the spells came every few years and I didn't give it much thought; I just continued on with my life as usual. During this time, I started to have premonitions. I kept getting the feeling that something life changing would happen when I turned 40.

This premonition would happen every 5 or more years. As I reached my late 30s, I would think about the premonition more often.

I believe it was a combination of the fall on my head, the mosquito bite on my arm and the bad diet that brought on the meningitis. Taking it full circle. I was in bed for around three days.

My spouse knew I was sick so she called my sister to have her check on me. My sister sent her son to see how I was doing and, on the third day, he took me to the hospital. I was checked out and released after one day, but I didn't feel any better.

I decided to stay at my sister's home for a while so that I could recover quickly. It was the week between Christmas and New Years. I remember feeling more ill every day. The illness was affecting my capacity to function properly, and my memory and my strength were declining daily. My decline escalated to the point where I needed my brother-in-law and my nephew to carry me down the stairs and drive me to the hospital emergency.

My mind was foggy, but I remember getting a needle in my spine, and then I blacked out. I was in a coma for four days. My family didn't know if I was going to survive. I could feel their presence in the room and hear them speaking. My body functions didn't work.

I tried to move my fingers but nothing happened. Thankfully, after four days, my eyes started to flutter, and soon I was able to open them and see my family.

Hospital Experience

I remember all the tubes and wires that were attached to my body. I spent one week in the intensive care unit before getting moved to a regular room.

The doctors would come daily and do all types of testing. One of the tests was running a small iron stick under my feet. Unfortunately, I didn't feel anything and when the tests were completed, the doctor told me that I had paralysis from my chest down. I couldn't even sit up on the bed without placing my arms on the bed beside me to keep me upright.

I knew my situation was dire but I had a strong determination to walk out of the hospital.

The first thing that came to my mind was, "I'm walking out of here."

After 2 weeks in the regular unit, the doctor told me that I was getting out. I felt great even though I still couldn't walk. What the doctor meant was, I was getting out of the regular unit and being transferred to rehab, where the therapist would start my treatments.

Two of the most important things I learned in the hospital were humility and the power of prayer, where people came together to pray for someone in need. The Universal Intelligence, the Source, God or whatever you choose to call it, is real energy that's omnipotent and miraculous.

That was the boost I needed to trigger the healing and my recovery.

My stay in rehab, for four weeks, was very humbling. I remember the nurse showing me how to transfer my body from the bed to the wheelchair, and vice versa. I had good upper body strength, so the transition was not as difficult for me as it was for others in the same condition. The only stipulation was that a nurse had to be present during the transfer.

On one particular day, I had just finished rehab and wheeled myself back to my room. I buzzed for the nurse and waited for twenty minutes. After a few more minutes of waiting, I decided to do the transfer myself. It was definitely a challenge without core or leg strength.

The transfer took about 20 minutes to get in the bed and sit up. Determination and persistence were key.

When the nurse finally arrived, she was amazed and a little baffled. She asked how I got into the bed. I told her I was buzzing for 25 minutes and didn't receive any assistance, so I did what I had to do.

She lectured me on the rules and subsequent danger of falling. From that day on, I did the transfer myself. I wanted to walk out of there, and I could feel how my strength was improving with each transfer.

I was also challenged by the injections I received twice a day in my abdominal area. The needles were to help eliminate blood clots in my legs. The needles were long and thick and the nurse used an overhand stab method of administration.

The needles continued for the first couple of weeks.

Eventually, I asked the physiotherapist what I needed to do to stop the daily needles. She said that I would need to walk at least 100 feet before the injections could stop.

Walking 100 feet became my goal. Using an electronic device, the therapist would activate the nerves in my legs. For several days, the stimulation therapy and rehab continued, and I was able to stand using parallel bars. I remember the first day standing. I thought I was standing straight and tall, but the therapist asked me to stand upright. When I did, I felt like I was going to fall backwards.

When I was finally able to stand upright, using the parallel bars, my therapist began to move my legs one at a time to simulate walking. By the third day, I could walk using the parallel bars to assist me. The next step was to use a walker, and soon I was walking 8 to 10 feet.

A few days later, when I was back in the rehab centre, the therapist had me do the walk, to see how many steps I could take. I started my walk and got tired halfway through. She asked me if I wanted to stop, and I said, "No, I want the needles to stop." With sheer determination, I walked 122 feet that day, and yes, the needles stopped. From that day on, I would walk the hallways in the hospital many times a day just to get more practice. I was determined to improve.

I was blessed to have some excellent therapists in rehab: an occupational therapist, to help me with everyday functioning like dressing and taking care of myself; a speech therapist, to help get my voice back and effectively use my brain; and a physiotherapist to help me walk again. These three young ladies impacted my recovery immensely, and I am eternally grateful.

During my four weeks in rehab, I consistently pushed myself. I thought about all the things I used to do before getting ill. I envisioned myself playing basketball, dancing, singing, putting on my socks and shoes, and just standing. Things we take for granted.

I believe that with the right mindset and attitude, you can truly do anything. I also believe that your mind plays a large part in your physical healing and well-being.

The hospital experience was humbling and a big part of why I wrote this book.

My hospital stay really changed my life. It gave me a new understanding and a powerful reminder not to take things for granted. During my hospital stay, I underwent tests, medications, speech, physical, and occupational therapy.

One of the procedures I experienced was needles in my abdominal area that caused scar tissue and resulted in lumps. The use of the catheter eventually affected how often I would use the bathroom.

All those drugs and toxins resulted in stress on my kidneys and liver, which would create an itching sensation that I couldn't scratch. This was one of the worst things I experienced, and it lasted for years. The itching sensation became less intense as time went by.

By the seventh week of hospitalization I was doubling my improvement. I was ready to get out of the hospital. On my release day, I was wheeled down to the exit and transferred to the car using a walker for assistance.

After leaving the hospital, I decided to go back to Canada to continue my rehab.

I stayed at my spouse's parents' home while recovering. Everything I did, felt like I was starting it for the first time. I couldn't even drive my car, which at the time was a manual transmission sports car.

That was the least of my problems. I had to start walking again without using a walker or a cane. I wanted to get back to my usual self and play basketball again, and do the things I used to do.

Walking without a walker came quickly. I couldn't see myself using a walker out in public, so I did everything in my power to improve as fast as possible. I remember the first couple of days, I would walk across the living room floor a few times. I would pick up the walker and walk carrying it. When I felt unstable, I would put it down and use it for balance.

After a few attempts carrying the walker, I decided to try it without the walker. The first try started out good, but I lost my balance and fell down. I was okay. I shook it off and did the walk again. I continued the practice until I was walking on my own.

The Next Challenge

My next challenge was to walk outside in public on my own, without any device to aid me. The walker only took a couple of days before I got rid of it. I wanted to go out, and I was not fully stable to walk around unassisted. The walking stick or cane was my tool of choice to help me get around. I used it for a couple of weeks before giving it up and walking on my own.

My physical structure was getting a lot better, and I made dramatic improvements.

I don't like taking medication drugs, so I went to a natural herbalist and some other alternative healers to assist me in my recovery.

I found an herbalist and an alternative therapy specialist. They both came up with the same diagnosis: liver and kidney stress.

I was put on several cleanses. My liver, kidneys, and even my blood went through this cleansing process. I must have cleansed for over 3 months.

The cleanses were focused on what I was eating and ingesting. I also received some tonics that helped with my recovery. During the cleanse, the itching sensation escalated.

That was the worst thing I ever experienced. The itching was unbearable. The only relief I could get was by having cool air on my skin and keeping calm. This went on for a few years, gradually getting better with time. After about two years, the itching would only happen when I was under high stress or the temperature was extremely hot.

After about a year, my hips started to give me trouble. I went to see a doctor and was diagnosed with avascular necrosis, which basically means that your hip joints are not getting proper blood supply. At that time, I was told that it was probably due to the fact that I had been on steroids to treat the meningitis while in the hospital.

After doing further research, I realized that it couldn't be what they originally stated, because I wasn't on that type of medication long enough to cause that problem.

I didn't like the thought of having to take medication, so I looked for alternative methods to alleviate the pain. One of the first things I tried was massage therapy. That was helpful, but I couldn't get a massage every day. My search continued for many months.

Chapter 3

The Birth of Transformation by Design

When I got to where I felt like my old self and could function properly, I started working at the YMCA.

I had a strange schedule when I was at the YMCA. Every Tuesday, I would work from 10 a.m. until 2 p.m., get off for three hours, and then start back at 5 p.m., until 10 p.m. closing time.

The head of the YMCA suggested that I start teaching the yoga class so that I could have a regular schedule.

I ended up taking a yoga fit training course from the YMCA. This certification allowed me to teach the yoga fit program. This was great for me because it gave me the opportunity to teach and practise at the same time.

When I was practising and teaching yoga, I found that my hips weren't as painful as they had been. My flexibility and function were greatly improved. After about one year of working at the YMCA, I decided to expand my horizons, and focus on ways to improve my own condition, and still keep assisting the members.

Transformation by Design came about because I was looking for ways to help myself recover and get back to a more healthy state. The techniques and training came to me when I started looking for better methods and techniques to help my recovery.

I was new to teaching yoga, but I had many years of training and experience in the fitness industry, and I wanted to share that knowledge with anyone I could help. Having this knowledge made me the primary person that YMCA members came to for instruction and advice.

I was the go-to guy to help you improve your fitness and wellness level. I found that yoga helped me alleviate a lot of my hip pain. This was a blessing in disguise to me. I continued doing yoga and started working with the stability balls. After a while, I decided to put together a workshop or seminar on how to use the stability balls.

At first, I thought a small class would be appropriate since we didn't have a lot of stability balls, and second, I wasn't sure how well it would be received. The sign-up sheet went out, and within a day or two, the class was full. I only expected 10 people, but to my surprise, there were already 15 signed and still more wanting to join. The number continued to grow. I informed the YMCA that there were only so many stability balls, so they went out and purchased a few more balls, and I did the class with 23 attendees.

I was very happy with the turnout and the feedback I received about the class. I decided that this would be excellent to teach to the firefighters in the town of Brantford. I put together a small workshop for the firefighters, at their stations. The last few stations came to the YMCA facility to participate in the program. It was received well by all, and that helped me with the creation of Transformation by Design.

Transformation by Design is my own holistic personal training business. This is what new fitness for active agers is all about. The whole concept started back in 2006, after getting back to a comfortable functional state. I wanted to create a program or training system that would help active agers like myself.

Most of the people were boomers, but a few were younger, some in their 20s. I wanted to help everyone age actively. When I instructed the class at the YMCA, in my stability ball/core training class, the participants would vary in age as well as gender. The class size was normally between 12–15 people, and we would train for one hour. I made the classes fun by doing creative things. I have always found the stability ball to be one of the best tools in the fitness industry. With a stability ball and some type of resistance tool, I can show anyone how to do a complete workout.

I was looking for more personal training work, but I was limited at the YMCA.

I continued working there for over a year. After leaving the YMCA, I came across an ad for a position in Toronto—a new fitness club that catered to the 40-plus crowd. I wanted to know more about this club, and possibly work there.

I applied for a position and, after a few months, I was called in for an interview. The interview went well and I was hired and started working in July.

Avalon Fitness Club

I enjoyed my time working at Avalon Fitness Club. The staff was a collection of knowledgeable, friendly, and caring individuals.

 My primary task was personal training. I also set up programs for new members, and instructed them on the proper use of the equipment. I was asked by the owner if I wanted to do some classes. I had the experience to instruct classes; however, I wanted to focus my attention on individual training.

After some contemplation, I decided to take on the challenge and create some classes. The first class I offered was a stability ball class.

This class was well received, so much so that the members wanted me to do more classes.

I started a circuit class. I was doing two classes per week. Monday was the stability ball class and Wednesday was the circuit class.

During my time at Avalon, I did everything a club owner would do. That was the concept the owner created for the club. Every one of the staff was responsible for all aspects of running the club: things like touring new members, signing agreements, instructing new members, and keeping the club looking clean and inviting at the same time.

I enjoyed the concept and it prepared me for running my own club. I thought the club would grow to a point where each of the employees could manage a different location.

I could envision good growth with Avalon, so I put my company on hold so that I could focus on the club's success.

The club ownership changed after a few years and I decided to get back to my own business. I still worked with a few members from the old club. I find it amazing when I look back and see some of the great relationships I have with my clients. Most of them are still with me today.

I have clients that have stayed loyal to me and my training methods for over 12 years. I feel blessed to have such wonderful people around me, whom I keep healthy, fit, and actively aging.

All of the knowledge, experience, and skills I have learned over the years have brought me to this place where I can now create new fitness programs for the active agers. The many challenges I had to go through made me stronger, and gave me a better understanding of the many things we all go through as we age.

This arena allowed me to share my experience and knowledge, in the hope that my clients and readers would learn something from it and improve their health situation.

I continued working at Avalon for a few years. Everything was going great. We had many events during my time there—things like book clubs, wine tastings, and some other social events. We also had a fashion show.

I loved the concept of having a place where you could go and exercise while enjoying the social aspects of aging. This was the ideal club for boomers and active agers.

I believed this was the type of fitness club that would expand all over the city.

However, after a few months and some financial issues, the club was sold. The new owner changed the main concept, and things started going south in a hurry.

I ended up leaving Avalon Fitness Club because my hours were reduced to part time. When we departed ways, I was running group fitness classes and boot camp at a studio, and doing personal training at Avalon, ten hours a week.

I realized it was time for me to refocus.

Studying to stay up-to-date with what was happening in the industry was a part of my plan. I am a lifelong learner who is always looking for ways to help enhance my life and the lives of my clients.

I was first introduced to the M.E.S. program by one of the other trainers at Avalon. After investigating many alternative methods and techniques, I decided to take the certification program and become a Medical Exercise Specialist.

With my M.E.S. training method, I was looking for people that were going through some of the things I experienced. I wanted to take personal training to a higher level.

M.E.S. was the missing link that gave me the knowledge and understanding of the medical professional working within the fitness industry. Doctor Mike Jones is the creator and originator of the M.E.S. program.

The Medical Exercise Program touched on all aspects of the rehab transition. You learned about the pathology of each medical condition, and what exercises you could do to manage that condition. You studied pathology to testing, to see if a client was ready to advance to the next phase, and everything in between. Learning how to bridge the gap between medical conditions and fitness, allowed me to put off hip surgery for years.

I wanted to get back to the way I was. Although I was getting older, I still felt like it was possible to make many improvements. I started doing some research on alternative healing methods. I was always into using my mind as a way to improve my physical being. Learning about energy and how everything is energy, and that energy cannot be created or destroyed. I found this concept amazing.

When I got the idea of using my mind to transform my body, that's when Transformation by Design was born. My concept was to take someone's energy and help them change it to a higher, stronger, and more positive energy.

My goal was to design a program that would help my clients achieve their desired results.

That is how the name came about. As time went on, I kept finding more alternative methods and techniques. After a few years, I had accumulated a great deal of skills from the knowledge and research I acquired.

My hip problems continued. By 2009 my hips were beginning to lock up on me when I was walking, plus I was experiencing excruciating pain on a daily basis.

Specialist Visit

I decided to go to a specialist to see if I could get a better understanding of my problem.

When the specialist saw the x-rays of my hips, he asked me, "How did you walk in here?" The x-rays looked bad, and the doctor explained to me that it wasn't a matter of whether I would need hip replacements; it was a matter of *when* I would need them.

I didn't want to undergo an operation. The thought of having an operation always scared me.

I did everything I could think of to avoid surgery. I managed my pain for eight years.

My stubborn nature kept me searching for alternative remedies and methods. After eight years of going through a pain level of between 5 and 9 on a daily basis, I finally gave in and decided to have the operation.

At that time, both of my hips were already in bad shape. My family doctor had retired and I was going to a clinic for check-ups and medical care. My new doctor made an appointment for me to see a specialist. Around the same time, I made an appointment to see an alternative pain specialist that worked with light therapy. Dr. Khan had many years of experience and had a great reputation for helping athletes.

When I went for my first consultation to see how he could help me, his reaction was similar to the specialist. He looked at my x-rays and said that there was nothing he could do for me. He told me I needed bilateral hip replacement surgery. He recommended Dr. Bogosh. I went to see Dr. Bogosh the following month, which was in February. When

I met Dr. Bogosh, I felt confident that he was the right doctor to do the surgery.

Dr. Bogosh has many years of experience and an exceptional team. We spoke about the surgery, and a date was set for the following month. This came as a surprise, since most people say they have to wait for 6 months to a year to get a surgery date.

In March 2017, the first operation was completed. The second one was scheduled for eight months later, in November. I wanted to wait to see how I reacted to the first surgery, and I wanted to give myself some time to process what was happening. I waited to see how quickly I would heal, before having the other hip surgery.

I was fortunate to have my operation scheduled for 9:00 a.m. The preparation for the surgery started the night before. I had to stop eating by 9:00 p.m. I also had to take a shower and use an antibacterial soap. This procedure was completed the last thing at night and the first thing in the morning.

I arrived at the hospital around 7 am. This was the normal protocol, since there was paperwork to complete, plus, the surgical team had to prep me before the doctor arrived.

Operation Time

I remember being wheeled down the hall to the operating room where I was transferred to the operating table. After that, I remember the nurse shaking me lightly to wake me up. I must have been very tired. I slept for 8 hours straight.

Most people would say that eight hours is normal. I hadn't slept 8 hours straight in the last 25 years, so it was unusual for me. When I woke up, I couldn't feel my legs and feet. I had to focus all of my attention on getting my toes to move. The whole ordeal took around 30 minutes. The more the drugs wore off, the better I moved. I was wheeled to my room around 5:45 p.m. My room was designated as semi-private however the other patient never showed up, so I had a private room.

My first night in the hospital was awful. I didn't have a phone or a television and my cell phone was almost out of power, and I didn't have a charger. I had to turn my phone off to preserve the power so that I could call home the next morning.

The first night, I didn't get much sleep. The second day was somewhat better. I finally got a television so that I could watch some shows. I also got my phone charger. By the next day, I felt better and was ready to get out of the hospital and go home.

On the Sunday afternoon, the physiotherapist came to the room and had me follow her to the testing centre. I had to walk up a couple of stairs, then across the floor and down a couple of stairs, and then turn around and go back to my starting spot.

The task was painful, but I managed to complete it. I was released about an hour later.

When I arrived home, my biggest challenge was getting up the stairs. With the help of a cane, I managed to get up the stairs and lay down in my bed.

My first few days at home were both physically and mentally challenging. Many things went through my mind. I wanted to get back to my life and do the things I was used to doing. The healing process would take a while; the incision had to heal, but I wanted to get moving as soon as possible.

During my first few weeks, I had some swelling and pain. I took the medication that was recommended. The medication was for infections and healing. As soon as the time was up, I stopped; I don't like taking medication when I know there are alternative foods that can give me the same results.

Learning to maneuver was challenging at first. My recovery was difficult because my other hip was beginning to lock more often.

After a week, I was able to go up and down the stairs using the handrail and a cane. A few days later, I was able to do the same task without a cane.

Once I could maneuver up and down the stairs by myself, I could conduct my weekly boot camp classes. My boot camp group has been with me for many years, so they knew the exercises, and that made it easy for me to instruct them on what to do, and to conduct the class effectively.

With some of my other clients, I would do a Skype call and instruct them using the computer. I did this until I was able to drive and go to my clients' homes again.

After a couple of months, I was back doing my classes and my in-home training. I continued the classes as usual and sat on a stability ball while instructing. It worked out well for everyone.

Second Operation

Fast forward eight months, and I'm ready for my second surgery.

This time around, I knew what to expect. The stress level wasn't as high, and I felt more confident having experienced it already. The second surgery was somewhat different.

I received less medication the second time around. The medication to help with the pain and to put me out was different. They gave me a smaller dosage. The first time, I had slept for over 8 hours. The second operation, I ended up waking during the operation.

I didn't feel any pain, but I could feel the vibration and pounding of the chiseling, where the rod was being inserted in my leg.

I was in my room by 4 p.m., instead of 5:30 p.m. like the first operation. The second surgery, I stayed in the hospital overnight and was released the following afternoon. Even though I got out early, the transitioning process was more difficult.

My healing took longer. Getting up and down the stairs was more challenging than the first time. The swelling was not as bad as the first time around, but getting around was more difficult.

Like the first time, I got back to training my clients after the first month. I took all the things I experienced, and I used the knowledge I had about exercise and rehab to put together a program for people dealing with hip surgery.

I know that having the two surgeries has helped me to have a better understanding of one's pre-operation anxiety. It's not just a physical thing, it's a mental and spiritual thing as well.

I always thought I would never have an operation. I did everything I could think of, and tried every alternative solution I could, but in the end, I had the operation and it has been a great thing for me. Remember, it took eight years for me to take that leap.

I hope this will help anyone going through the same experience, to get some comfort in knowing that everything will be okay. Both having an experienced doctor and preparing yourself before the operation are necessary to getting the best results and the quickest recovery.

When you follow the techniques in this book, and you raise your vibrational level, things will fall into place, and your recovery will be just how you visualized it.

You may be wondering how this concept could apply to you. Believe me it does. I have at least two significant examples of how the universe and the power of your mind can and does influence a lot of the challenges you may be experiencing.

My first example goes back to when I was in the hospital in Rochester NY with meningitis. I made reference to the situation in a previous chapter but just to recap. I was in the hospital and in a coma for the better part of a week.

The doctors diagnosed paralysis, however my mind and vibration said I'm walking out of here.

The interesting thing was I felt certain about what I was saying to myself.

I had an unshakeable confidence in the expected results. I believe that is what you need to have to get the results you want. The right mind set is the beginning to accomplishing your goal and getting the results you want.

I had to put in a lot of physical work and determination to get the results I wanted, but it was all worth it.

The second example was more recent. In March of 2019 I went for my yearly physical exam. My blood work was good, however the doctor was concerned as my PSA level had changed drastically. My Dad passed away from prostate cancer the year before.

My Doctor made an appointment for me to see an oncologist.

The Specialist told me that because the level of my PSA rose, I might need a biopsy to see if there was any cancer. He explained the procedure, which didn't sound very inviting. He said we will do another blood test before we do the biopsy.

The biopsy was scheduled in 6 weeks, so I had some time to work on raising my vibration. I waited two weeks before I went for my second blood test. During that two weeks I visualized and did all the things necessary to raise my vibration and frequency.

I kept saying to myself, my blood work is going to come back positive and I will not need to do a biopsy. I had my blood test and the following day I received a call from the doctor's office to say that my biopsy had been cancelled.

When I saw the doctor he told me that my PSA level had gone back to normal. The year before it was .73 and in 2019 it was 10. Following my vibrational raising techniques and visualizations my PSA level went down to .68, which was even better than the year before.

The above examples are to show you how the mind and body work together holistically united for your betterment.

I have other techniques that I use to help increase my frequency, energy and vibration. I often use subliminal and hypnotic techniques. Affirmations are also part of my daily ritual.

This book is for all active agers. I will share the knowledge and experiences that I used to get back on my feet, plus the things I do now to stay healthy and fit. I will also share some of the techniques that will help you get into the right vibration, at the right frequency, and in the mindset you need to be in to be the best version of you.

My company, Transformation by Design, was originally created for holistic personal training. It has evolved into managing medical conditions with exercise and alternative therapies.

I have put together a series of things I personally do. I'm an old-school dude. I grew up in the 60s and 70s, when you had fun outside with friends, good music, and old remedies. I still enjoy listening to my old school music. The music is a great reminder of my experiences, and it's just fun to listen to.

Chapter 4

It All Starts With a Breath

Breath is life, and if you're still breathing, you can improve. That was part of my experience when I was in the hospital. I had machines working for me to give me that breath, but once I could take my own breath, that's when everything turned around.

No matter what level of fitness you're at, if you can still breathe, you can be helped. It doesn't matter if you're bedridden or in a wheelchair; there's a starting point and breathing is it.

To burn anything you need three things: 1) fuel (body fat in this case); 2) Heat (our body heats up with movement); 3) oxygen (the air we breathe in).

Most weight loss programs focus on diet by decreasing the amount of fuel or fat that is burned. Other programs focus on heating up the body with exercise to produce more fat burning. I haven't seen many focus on increasing the amount of oxygen we intake. When you increase your oxygen intake, you get rid of 80% of the toxins in your body.

Deep Breathing

Most of us breathe too shallow. We often use the upper part of the lungs, which can only take in small amounts of air, instead of using the lower part, which can take in much more air. This shallow breathing is both 'caused by' stress and anxiety and 'causes' stress and anxiety.

Most of us only exchange half a litre of air with each inhale and exhale cycle. Twelve cycles a minute means we get around 6 litres of fresh air per minute. These 6 litres include around 1.2 litres of pure oxygen. If you practice effective deep breathing, you can exchange up to six times more air. That means you can actually take in up to SIX LITRES OF PURE OXYGEN per minute, instead of 1.2 litres.

If oxygen deprivation is the main cause of poor metabolism and obesity, then you can see how important effective deep breathing is. The final goal is to have your body breathe deeply and effectively 24 hours a day, 7 days a week, without you even having to think about it.

One of the first methods I used was taking deep breaths. I would inhale for approximately four to five seconds, hold the breath, and then exhale it out. I would keep doing this throughout the day, and I would feel the improvements every day. In a couple of weeks, I was able to inhale for 10 seconds, fill my lungs with air, hold that breath for 10 seconds, and exhale it. I kept on using this technique because it was working well and it helped to energize my whole being.

That was the starting technique. From there, I incorporated a new breathing technique. This technique was called the "1-4-2 breathing exercise." This is how it works: You inhale for a count of 1; you then hold the breath for a count of 4, and then exhale for a count of 2. Example: Inhale for 5 seconds, hold the breath for 20 seconds, and exhale the breath for 10 seconds.

This is a very powerful technique and should not be taken lightly. Start slow, and give yourself and your body time to adjust to this technique. You may feel dizzy or light headed if you attempt this technique too quickly. Give yourself a few months to get to "5-20-10." In six months of regular practice, you will be healthier, have a better functioning set of lungs, and your energy will be greatly improved. (Like all techniques in this book, it is best to consult your doctor before attempting any of them).

This is a great technique to help improve your abdominal area as well. When you do the exhale part of the technique, you should tighten your abs to push all of the air out of your lungs. By tightening and holding your contracted abdominal area, it will help work the muscles on a deeper level, and you will improve as you continue using the technique. The best thing about these techniques is that they can be done in a lying, sitting, or standing position. With continuous practice, you will be doing them on autopilot.

Before you know it, you will be breathing better, generating more energy, and improving your overall health. By the time this happens, you will be ready for more exercises and techniques that will keep you evolving and transforming to the best version of you.

Once you have mastered the above techniques, it is time to start some more advanced techniques.

This breathing exercise is similar to the ones you have mastered. Start by taking a long, deep breath, and fill your abdominal area and your lungs as much as possible. Inhale for 1–10 seconds or whatever you can do. I started doing this exercise by inhaling for 2 seconds and then I would increase it by 1 or 2 seconds each day.

When you do the exercise, first fill your abdominal area, then your lungs; then picture filling all of your extremities with air, the way you would if you were a blow-up doll. On the exhale, start by emptying your extremities first, then your lungs, and finally your abdominal area. You will probably get a slight buzz or dizzy feeling. This full range breathing technique will help to cleanse toxins from your body, and will increase your energy as well.

When you perform these exercises on a regular basis, you will notice an added sense of awareness.

Breathing

The best way to increase your energy level is by breathing in clean, fresh air. We live in a time and place where the air is full of pollution and toxins. Take some time to go to the park, or someplace where there is lots of trees and nature. Trees help to clean the air, and produce oxygen for humans to breathe. You need to get some fresh air. Take a trip, go up north or down south. Wherever you decide to go, make sure there's clean, fresh air to breathe.

Doing the exercises mentioned in the previous pages, will work best in a clean air environment. The benefits will be greatly multiplied.

However, if you cannot get away to some clean air environment, then I suggest you look into air cleaners and air purifying machines. The better your air, the better you will feel and the healthier you will be. Another way to improve your breathing is by practicing qigong, yoga, and tai chi.

Water, Like Air, Can Be So Wonderful and So Devastating

Water and air are very beneficial. Water is needed to live and you can only survive without water for a few days. Just being hydrated can improve your brain function, your skin, your metabolism and so many other important things. Too much water and you can drown.

Air has many benefits as well. I believe air is more important than water. You can only survive without air or oxygen for minutes. When you receive the correct amount of oxygen, your brain functions better. Breathing helps release toxins from your body. Air or oxygen helps your heart function and keeps you alive. Too much air can be devastating. A hurricane or a tornado can end life very quickly.

Like I said in the beginning, water, like air, can be so wonderful and so devastating.

I have some examples of techniques and exercises to help you get the amount of air or oxygen you need to function at your best. Just walking or doing any cardio training will help you breathe deeper and produce more oxygen. Some people prefer to just meditate and do deep breathing exercises.

I prefer qigong because it's not complicated or strenuous, and it's easy to learn. You don't have to be in perfect health to get started.

I started a few years ago and I didn't go to a dojo or a martial arts studio. I purchased a DVD program that came with the online version as well. The program, "Discover Qi," by Lee Holden, got me started and I have been using the program and sharing it with my clients ever since.

I like the way the program is presented; it's easy to follow and Lee explains it in a modern layman's way. A young child could follow along and reap the benefits.

This program is wonderful for boomers and any active ager. For anyone with mobility issues, and/or suffering from pain, then qigong might be a smart place to start.

Some of the changes you will probably experience are a heightened sense of awareness and a holistic consciousness that will keep you coming back for more. This new feeling will increase your vibration and energy level. Your health, wealth, and relationships will benefit as you stay on your transformational journey.

Meditation is another way to practise and improve your breathing skills. Most of the skills for breathing are threefold, meaning they will help you on a physical, mental, and spiritual level. When you combine these three, they add up to energy. I like to use this example: Ice = Physical; Water = Mental; Steam = Spirit.

Breathing is your body's way of transferring oxygen to the cells. This transforms your body to a higher vibration and increases your energy. Breathing is a vital part of the whole being; use it as a starting point. Incorporate the other techniques from this book to transform your life to the way you want it to be, by your own design—the Transformation by Design way—so you can be the best version of you that there is.

Chapter 5

You Are What You Eat

In this chapter, we're going to talk about food. What and when should you be eating? I'm sure you have seen many commercials about weight management. Some talk about exercise and the new equipment that will help you lose weight or inches in a few weeks.

There are new fad diets being introduced all the time. What should you do? What diet or exercise should you use?

To tell you the solution in its simplest form, I would say "move more and eat less." The movement should be in a structured form that allows you to use all of your body in a functional manner. The exercise doesn't have to be difficult or strenuous, but consistency will give you the results you want. Take a look at the chapter on movement, and you will see some easy-to-do movements and exercises that will get you going and keep you improving.

Nutritious eating is more complex but is still doable. Science and opinions about nutrition and exercise change daily. Everybody is different; we all have different needs and goals. You may have a different reaction to food than a sibling or friend. It all depends on your individual food sensitivities.

One of the things I have been telling my clients for years is to listen to your body. It knows what it needs and what it can do.

Eating a balanced, nutritious diet is a must in order to get proper nutrition and good energy. Your body also needs protein and fat to function at an optimal level. A multivitamin can be beneficial if you are not eating high nutrient rich foods.

With the hectic pace of life, most people are too busy to eat well. They substitute good nutrient rich foods with fast nutrient depleted junk food.

This type of food only fills space and you end up feeling bloated and hungry in a short time. As the saying goes, most fat people are starving. That might sound crazy; however, without the proper nutrients, your body tries to fill the void by eating more unhealthy food, which creates a cycle and starts a bad habit.

That's how overweight people become obese. The habit of eating junk food becomes an obsession that your brain uses to justify the overeating. An addiction is formed when you need food because your feelings are hurt or you are disappointed about some situation.

The cycle needs to be changed and the way to change it is by having an awareness of what's happening to you. Awareness is curative; when you know there's a problem, you do something about it. Start by implementing some of the transformational habits.

One of the best ways to overcome a bad habit is to use a journal. Keep a record of all the foods you are eating, and everything that is going into your mouth. This will give you the awareness of how good or bad your diet is.

This awareness will be the starting point.

Take it a step at a time. Record your dietary habits for one day and then go over it to see what types of foods you are consuming. This simple task takes discipline, but it helps you improve and will get you on the right track.

To make the recording easier, get a small note book and put the date at the top.

The first entry should be breakfast; note the time of day

Example:

Breakfast: Cereal with fruit, coffee, toast
Time: 8:00 a.m.

Time: 10:00 a.m. Smoothie

Lunch: Salad with chicken, water, slice of pie
Time: 12:30 p.m.

Time: 2:00 p.m. Yogurt with fruit, some mixed nuts

Dinner: Steamed veggies and baked fish, small salad
Time: 6:30 p.m.

Evening: Herbal tea, with some cookies
Time: 8 p.m.

The above is an example of how to space out your eating time, and how you should record what you ate.

For anyone looking to lose weight, I suggest you have 8oz of water about 45 minutes before each meal. This will help suppress your appetite and remove toxins from your body.

When you eat is very important. Following an eating schedule will help keep your blood sugar stable instead of peaking and crashing. Eating on a regular cycle will help improve your metabolism by challenging it to keep processing calories, rather than storing them. Your body will not go through the feast or famine state that can cause fat storage.

Below is a list of some foods that you can incorporate into your diet.

Fruits:

Medium apple	Mango
Apricots	Nectarine
Banana	Orange
Cantaloupe	Papaya
Cherries	Peach
Dried fruit	Pear
Fresh squeezed fruit juice	Raspberries
Grapefruit	Strawberries
Grapes	Tangerine
Kiwi	Watermelon

Vegetables:

Asparagus	Lettuce
Beets	Marinara sauce
Bok choy	Mushrooms
Broccoli	Peas
Brussels sprouts	Peppers
Cabbage	Spinach
Carrots	Sprouts
Cauliflower	Squash
Celery	String beans
Cucumber	Tomatoes
Eggplant	V-8 Juice
Kale	

Do your best to get 3–5 servings of the above fruits and veggies into your diet every day, and before long you will see the benefits.

Eating

"You are what you eat" is a very popular and powerful statement. I believe this is a true statement and if you adhere to it you will reap the positive benefits of a good nutritious diet. You might be wondering what you should eat, how much, what time and how many times per day.

These questions, and the saying, "you are what you eat," go back to old-school days. Human beings have been trained or conditioned to eat at certain times of the day. The training started when you were young. You had to get up in the morning around 7 a.m. to get ready for school, have breakfast around 8 a.m., and make your way to school for 9 a.m.

You got your first recess around 10:15–10:30 a.m. Lunch was at noon, for about 1 hour. Then around 2:15–2:30 p.m., you would get your last recess; and at 3:30 p.m., you were finished school.

When you got home, you did your chores and your homework, and you had your dinner between 5 and 7 p.m. That was the old-school schedule that most of us followed.

That schedule and system has programmed most of us to eat at certain times of the day. When you got older and started working, you followed a similar schedule. You might have started earlier or worked later, but the programming remained.

The time you eat is important, but what you eat is even more important. If you're looking to lose weight, you should think about juicing or eating fruits first thing in the morning. This will give your body the proper nutrients and carbohydrates to increase your energy so that you can function until your next meal.

Your snack meals should be a mixture of carbs, proteins, and good fats. Something as simple as having some nuts or some vegetables/fruits with a helping of protein is good. There are many recipes and food suggestions online, or you can go to a bookstore and pick out some recipes. The main thing is to make sure your food is nutritious, non-processed, clean and something that you actually like.

How often should you eat? I prefer smaller meals more often and I also believe that you should stop eating 2–3 hours before you go to bed. This allows your body the right amount of time to digest your food and eliminate waste.

While you are sleeping, your body will be rejuvenated, building muscle and burning fat. Your body should be in a fasting mode for at least 12 hours. An example of that would be to get up at 7 a.m. and eat whenever you want until 7 p.m. that night.

As you may have noticed, I did not say to eat *whatever* you want. I said *whenever* you want, within the 12-hour time frame. Using this method makes it easier and more enjoyable than sticking to a diet. You shouldn't have to feel like somebody's looking over your shoulder every time you want to eat. Feel free to enjoy your food, but be sensible with your choices. Remember: "You are what you eat."

 Making these little changes of fasting for 12 hours, and eating anytime you like within the other 12 hours, will get you some measurable results in a week or two. This will help you lose some extra weight. However, if you eat high nutrient rich foods, and do the transformation workout, your results will be better and faster.

Try it, you'll like it, and you will feel the increase in your energy as well. Everything is linked together—your energy, your thoughts, your breathing, your movements, and nutrition all come full circle to get you to be the best version of you.

This all happens through discipline and action. I like to do challenges for 30 days because it puts me in a state of commitment, and it's doable.

Everyone wants to be healthy and eat good, nutritious foods but most are unsure about what to eat.

Since we all have different body types, genetics and tastes, the choice is yours for the type of food you prefer. Here is a list of the things you should try to avoid: foods that come in boxes, cans, or some sort of packaging. These foods normally contain high levels of sodium to keep them preserved, so check the labels on these types of foods before buying them.

The next thing is, the more fruits and vegetables you eat, the better off you will be and feel.

We in North America have been conditioned to eat meat with every meal. It's on the food chart and every ad you come across is selling some delicious looking burger or some attractive food that makes you want to jump off the wagon and eat.

Don't do it! Stick to your plan and concentrate on the weight you want to be. Refocus your mind and think about how great you will look and feel.

One thing you might want to consider is doing a fast.

A fast is a great way to lose the unwanted fat, plus it helps rejuvenate your digestive system by giving it some needed rest.

There are many types of fasts that you can do, but before doing anything, always consult your doctor or health care professional.

When doing a fast, it is best to prepare yourself. Don't try to do a 7-day fast your first try. Work up to it. Here is an example: If you are used to eating 3 meals a day, plus a few snacks, then you should start by eliminating the snacks and start drinking water instead. When you have accomplished that task for 3–7 days, then it might be time to try skipping one meal each day. The first week, you might skip breakfast. Then the next week, you skip lunch; and the third week, you skip dinner. When you reach this stage, it will be easier to go for a period of time without food. As an example, eat only between 1 and 7 p.m., or from 2–8 p.m., eat as much as you like, but only nutritious foods, and fast for the remainder of the day. This type of fast works for most people because they are sleeping for a large part of the fasting time.

The next type of fast is one where you are only having liquids—but no alcohol, soda, or any drink with lots of sugar. Juicing or having a smoothie is a great way to get all of your nutrients while reducing your hunger.

When you have accomplished this stage of your fasting, you can try doing a water fast. Try the water fast for 1–2 days and if you feel good with the process, continue. When you reach the 4- day mark, you will feel euphoric and have a sense of clearness. Do this fast for 4–7 days, and if you will feel good and accomplish your task, go back to juicing and gradually bring back some solid foods. You will be happy with the results if you follow the process as stated above.

When you decide to fast or change your diet, you should think of ways to implement those changes.

A great way to start is to pick a bad habit that you want to stop and substitute it with a good habit. As an example, if you have coffee first thing in the morning and you want to reduce the amount of coffee or eliminate it, try having a glass of water first and then wait 15 minutes to a half an hour before having your coffee. Continue this process for a week.

Making a small change every day, by adding 5 minutes more between drinking your water and your coffee, will have substantial benefits. By the end of the week you will be up to one hour between your water and your coffee. Imagine in 2 weeks you might make it a habit and stick with it.

Whatever habit you want to change, you can do it. Most people make New Year's resolutions or set goals they want to accomplish. I don't know what the statistics are, but I'm sure a large percentage of people who have resolutions and goals don't stick to them for over a month.

Why don't they stick to their goals? The average person doesn't know what they want. You have to know what you want and where you are going before you can start. You have to deal with each day as it comes. The first thing is to make a commitment to yourself. Write it down, sign it and place it where you can see it every day. A good place might be beside your tooth brush or on the mirror. We are in 2020, so on your phone or computer would make the most sense.

The more you see your goals, the deeper the impression will be on your mind, and the quicker it will manifest. Discipline is your friend, so commit, write your food goal down, and follow it every day. Make it your challenge for 30 days, but do it one day at a time.

By the time you realize it, the 30 days are over, and you have completed your challenge. Plus, you formed a new habit, which will make you feel better, improve your health, and raise your vibration to a higher level.

Chapter 6

Let It Flow

Some quick facts about water:

Fact number one: Only 57% of adults drink more than 4 cups of water per day. Women should have about 9 cups per day, and men about 13 cups. This all depends on weight and size.

Fact two: People who drink more water, eat more fruits and veggies, exercise more, and eat less junk food.

There are many different kinds of water, but they can be separated into four major groups:

Odourless, tasteless water. These are the purest waters, and the mineral content is quite low. Evian water, for example, is the benchmark used by professionals in the bottled water industry.

Odourless water that has taste. These are the classic spring waters. Minerals like calcium, magnesium, or sodium result in a slight flavour.

Water with odours and no taste. These are also classic spring waters. In contrast to the waters of the second group, they contain minerals like Sulphur, which gives them a strong characteristic odour. These waters are not sold commercially but are available directly from the spring at the thermal spa.

Water that has both taste and odour. This is tap water; the presence of chlorine gives it both odour and taste.

Despite all their characteristics, these waters can be drunk by human beings with no ill effects.

*(The above info was taken from the book, *The Water Prescription*, by Christopher Vasey.)

The hydrating capacity of water can be enhanced by adding a structuring agent. The structuring formula is composed of ionic minerals that organize and reduce the water molecules, holding them together in small clusters, to facilitate their flow through the cell membranes.

Infusions

The leaves from plants, such as mint, basil and thyme give a pleasant aroma and flavour to the water in which they are steeped, which makes infusion a satisfying alternative for people who don't enjoy drinking plain water.

Below is a list of some recipes that can be used to infuse your water.

SIX SIMPLE RECIPES

Some infused water recipes using a 32-ounce container:

#1) 4 orange slices, 10 grapes (halved), 4 fresh basil sprigs

#2) Granny apple, sliced into 8 pieces; 5 fresh ginger slices; 2 lemon grass sticks

#3) 5 cucumber slices, 2 thyme sprigs, 4 tangerine slices

#4) Grapefruit slices, 2 rosemary sprigs, 3 small jalapeño slices with no seeds

#5) 8 pear slices, 1 cinnamon stick, half a vanilla bean

#6) 1 green tea bag, 2 fresh mint sprigs, 20 pomegranate arils, crushed

(The above information was taken from *The Water Prescription*, by Christopher Vasey.)

Stay Hydrated

Make sure you keep a pitcher or two of plain water or infused water in the fridge. When you prepare your day or week in advance, things will run smoother, and you will get all your tasks accomplished. Your goal is to increase your hydration level. When you have the recommended amount of water ready, then it's easy to do.

Drink a pitcher or two of water every day for a week. After one week, extend it to two weeks, then one month. When you get this far, it becomes a habit and you will see the benefits: how much better your body is functioning, and how much better your skin looks. You will want to continue on your transformation journey.

At this stage, you must intake enough water to keep hydrated so that your body functions at optimal level. One of the benefits you will notice is weight reduction. The combination of oxygen, from breathing properly and water, will help burn more fat and assist your body with eliminating toxins, and help you feel and look better.

You are constantly losing water from your body, primarily via urine and sweat. To prevent dehydration you need to drink adequate amounts of water.

There are many different opinions on how much water you should be drinking every day.

Health authorities commonly recommend eight 8-ounce glasses, which equals about two litres or half a gallon. This is called the 8×8 rule and is very easy to remember.

However, some health gurus believe that you need to sip on water constantly throughout the day, even when you're not thirsty.

As with most things, this depends on the individual. Many factors (both internal and external) ultimately affect your need for water.

This article takes a look at some water intake studies to separate fact from fiction, and explains how to easily match water intake to your individual needs:

Does Water Intake Affect Energy Levels and Brain Function? How Much Water Should You Drink?

Many people claim that if you don't stay hydrated throughout the day, your energy levels and brain function start to suffer.

One study in women showed that a fluid loss of 1.36% after exercise impaired mood and concentration, and increased the frequency of headaches.

Other studies showed that mild dehydration (1–3% of body weight) caused by exercise or heat can harm many other aspects of brain function.

Keep in mind that just 1% of body weight is a fairly significant amount. This happens primarily when you're sweating a lot.

Mild dehydration can also negatively affect physical performance, leading to reduced endurance.

Mild dehydration caused by exercise or heat can have negative effects on both your physical and mental performance.

Does Drinking a Lot of Water Help You Lose Weight?

There are many claims that increased water intake may reduce body weight by increasing your metabolism and reducing your appetite.

According to two studies, drinking 17 ounces (500 ml) of water can temporarily boost metabolism by 24–30%.

Water is the essence of life, and since our bodies are approximately 60% water, we need to stay hydrated to function at our optimal level. The type of water is also very important. You should have an awareness of the many toxins in tap water as well as bottled water that you may be purchasing. One of the best ways to get good clean water is to use a filter. Here is a list of a few of the water filters I have used:

1) Nikken
2) Tyent
3) Brita

I presently use a Tyent water purifying system, which is connected under the sink in the kitchen. This type of water system was chosen for some good reasons. This system has eight settings: 3 levels of alkaline, 3 levels of acidity, one regular H20 filter, and a turbo level. For drinking purposes, the alkaline is best for your health. The acidic is best used for washing fruits and veggies, and the higher acidity is best for cleaning purposes (ideally to help eliminate bacteria and viruses around the house).

You now have a better idea of how much water you need, and the type of water you should be drinking. The temperature of the water is another factor. Below is a comparison between cold water vs warm water.

COLD WATER: The body has to expend energy to warm up the water in order to use it. It helps to cool down the body after exercise but it constricts blood vessels and reduces hydration and absorption ability. It solidifies fats from food and causes the body to work harder to digest.

WARM WATER: Soothes blood vessels and allows better hydration. It helps move fats along, reducing the risk of clogged arteries, and allows better digestion. It helps to flush the kidneys and improve bowel movement. When experiencing a fever, warm water reduces the body's effort to fight the virus.

17 benefits of drinking water:

1) Supports heart health
2) Improves circulation
3) Increases waste removal
4) Flushes out toxins
5) Nutrient absorption
6) Increases energy and alertness
7) Supports healthy weight loss
8) Improves complexion
9) Supports muscle building
10) Enhances brain function

11) Boosts immune system

12) Prevents headaches

13) Prevents kidney stones

14) Prevents cramps

15) Supports joints

16) Prevents backache

17) Prevents bad breath

Some studies have shown that you can make your water healthier by blessing it or saying positive words to it. In a study conducted by Dr. Masura Emoto, it shows how water reacts to conscious frequencies. Take a minute and google the study and you will see for yourself the effects of the experiment; with some visual proof, it's quite amazing.

Using the above information, and taking some time to speak positive words or blessings to the water you are about to consume, will help your overall health. This is part of the new fitness for active agers.
The holistic approach brings this concept full circle—mind, body, and spirit. Using your body, and taking your mind to a positive loving level will increase your vibration and spiritual level. Speaking the words to your water will be the positive blessing your body needs to become and stay healthy.

Chapter 7

Movement Is Key

Your mindset is where you need to start. Change your focus, and visualize yourself at the weight you want to be. When you start to focus on your desired outcome, your brain begins to look for ways to help you find a solution and ultimately, you become more aware of what you are putting into your mouth. This triggers your brain to start forming new habits.

The same way a bad habit was formed, a good habit can be formed. When you go back in this book, you will find simple things you need to do to get back to your best self or become your best self.

I find qigong an excellent way to keep your mind, body, and spirit healthy. When you incorporate fasting with qigong, you begin to understand what optimal health is, and what Transformation by Design is all about.

As the saying goes, sitting is the new smoking. How many of the boomers who were so active in the old days are still active today? How many are in jobs where they spend most of their time sitting?

The main reason for the statement above is that by sitting for an extended time, your body is in a position that shortens your Psoas muscle, or more commonly known as your hip flexors.

The hip flexor is the only muscle in your body that connects the upper body to your lower body. When your hip flexors are tight, they create a lot of problems. Things like lower back pain, hip issues and issues with knees and even ankles are just some of the challenges you will have to deal with, if your hip flexors are shortened from sitting too long.

This is why you are reading this book, so that you can transform your life and improve your health with the techniques and exercises I shared.

As we all know, stagnant water, just like a sedentary lifestyle, attracts bacteria, toxins and disease. Your body has to be moving to be healthy and clean. Let's look at some ways to help you start moving again. One of my New Year's resolutions was to increase my cardio. I have a stationary bike, and I know that doing 12 minutes of interval training on the bike is equivalent to walking on a treadmill for 45 minutes (without the interval part of it).

The intervals play a significant part in this exercise. This training can be done on a bike, treadmill, or elliptical machine and if you don't have any of these pieces of equipment, you can march in place or jog in place.

This is how it works. Start by doing 30 seconds of any of the above exercises for the first day. Every day you need to add 30 seconds. The first 30 seconds will be at regular speed, and the next 30 seconds at a more intense speed. The whole process should take 7 weeks. It seems like a long time to do just 12 minutes but if you have been sedentary for a few years, you will appreciate going slow and improving gradually.

Start on Monday by doing 30 seconds at regular speed and 30 seconds at high intensity.

On Tuesday, you add 30 seconds at regular speed; and on Wednesday, you add 30 seconds at high intensity. Continue this method for the week, and by Friday, you will be doing two and a half minutes.

On the following Monday, start where you left off, at 2 1/2 minutes. Keep adding 2 1/2 minutes each week for 7 weeks, until you reach 12 minutes. When you reach the 7-week mark, you will feel awesome for sticking to the routine, and for moving more than you have in the last few years. The main thing is to be consistent; don't give up. You will feel happy to accomplish this feat. In seven weeks, you have turned a simple exercise into a habit that will help you for the rest of your life.

Now that we have the cardio conquered, let's look at some resistance training. My go-to exercise for upper body training is push-ups. I know a lot of you can't do push-ups, so let's learn some simple techniques and master them. Let's start with wall push-ups. Walk up to the wall and place your hands on it. Step back 1–2 feet and bring your chest to the wall, and push away so your arms are straight; do about 5 reps at first, and build up to doing 10–15 reps at a time.

When you have mastered the wall push-up, it's time to get a stability ball and start doing ball push-ups. Use the ball to support your body. Lay on top of the ball in a prone position, and go out as far as you can comfortably so that you can do a few push-ups. As your strength increases, you can go out a little further, which will make the push-ups more challenging. When you can roll out far enough that the ball is at your knees, you can try doing push-ups on your knees on a mat.

When you can do 10 knee push-ups, move on to regular push-ups, with toes on the floor and hands on the floor. Keep your core level, with no arching, and work your way up to 10 push-ups. When you can do 10 push-ups easily, try adding one push-up a day until you reach 25 push-ups. The next goal is to do 25 push-ups in the morning and 25 more in the evening.

One of the first challenges is to do four sets of 25 push-ups throughout the day, which will be 100. When you reach this level, you can join the 100 push-ups per day challenge for 30 days. By the time you reach this point, your upper body will be much stronger, and you will feel like taking on more challenges.

The next exercise is for your lower body. Let's start with chair squats: Sit in a chair with your feet flat on the floor, cross your arms over your chest, and stand up. Now sit back down and repeat for 5–10 reps. If you find it difficult to do this because of injury etc. start by doing leg extensions. Slowly extend your leg out so that your toe is pointing to the ceiling and your calf is parallel to the floor. Start with 10–15 reps per leg; as you improve, use a light weight or resistance band to make it more challenging.

By now, you are comfortable doing chair squats, your leg strength has improved and you're feeling pretty good. This is a great time to try some ball squats. The stability ball is one of my favourite tools. This is an excellent piece of equipment for doing wall squats.

Find an area where you can place the ball on the wall, and put your back on the ball. Place the ball at your lower back and hip area. From here, you need to step forward about one to two feet so that you're leaning back on the ball. When you are in this position, try doing a squat so that you're in a sitting position.

This is the position that you need to work from. Start by doing 5 squats, going down to a seated position, and standing back up; that is one rep. Do 10 reps and, on the 10th rep, stay in the sitting position for 10 seconds. The next set, complete 9 reps and hold for 9 seconds. Continue this sequence until you reach 5 reps.

When you complete this exercise for your quads, the next body part is your calves or lower legs. Turn around so that the ball is at your chest. The next step is to go on your toes. Do heel raises for 10 reps, and hold for 10 seconds in the up position. Continue counting down to 5 reps, and hold for 5 seconds, the same way you did with your legs. This is an excellent exercise for your lower body, and it will give you many health benefits.

We have two more areas we need to work on—back and abs—which make up our core. To start, you must build strength. The goal is to do pull-ups or chin-ups. To most people, that seems impossible. You may say, "I'm well past my prime, so why attempt that exercise?" Start slowly and set your goals. You don't have to do pull-ups to improve your strength, but it would give you bragging rights and increase your confidence.

Start with some simple movements like picking something up. Let's call it the one-arm row. Get a light weight, about 5–10 pounds. You can use a can or a heavy pot with a handle, something you can grip. A set of dumbbells would be ideal, or some tubing or bands that have some resistance. A chair is needed. Place the chair in front of you so that you can place your hand in the seat. Hold your weight with one hand, step back from the chair about 1–2 feet, and bend over with your back flat. Reach toward the opposite side, between your foot and the chair leg, pause, and pull the weight back slowly.

Bring the weight towards your arm pit. This is a one-arm row. It's an excellent exercise to strengthen your back muscles as well as your core and arms. This is just a small sample of how to use what you already have to transform your body. I can assist you in designing the program that's tailored to you.

Now you have some exercises that you can do to help strengthen your chest, back, and legs. Let's take a look at your core—the main part, your centre the abdominal area. This is one of the most popular body parts that every article and fitness magazine talks about. Abdominal muscles—how to flatten them, how to get that six-pack, and just how to generally reduce fat around the mid-section.

Some of the techniques I have shown you in this book should be helping you with your strength and stability, and accelerating the fat burning process. You still need to do some form of exercise to strengthen and build the muscles in the abdominal and core area.

Start by getting a stability ball or a chair, placing a mat on the floor, and putting your legs on the ball or on the chair. Make sure you are at a 90-degree angle, with your calves touching the ball or chair.

Start by reaching towards the ball or the chair, and touching it on both sides at the same time, then returning to start position.

Do 10 repetitions, and hold on the tenth one for 10 seconds, followed by 9 repetitions, and holding for 9 seconds. Continue this pattern until you reach five reps, holding for 5 seconds.

When performing this exercise, make sure your chin is not down towards your chest. Visualize that you have a ball under your chin; this will help you to keep your head in the correct position. When doing any abdominal exercise, it is best to keep your spine aligned. When doing crunches, place your hands behind your head to support the weight of your head and to take some stress off of your neck.

Do not do old-school sit-ups. Remember the ones we did in school? Someone would hold your legs, or you would place your feet under the bar for support, and you would perform full range sit-ups. This style of sit-up is ineffective. Injuries can occur when doing this exercise. A crunch is an exercise for the abdominal muscles, which when performed correctly will give you great results.

To do the crunch correctly, lay on your back with your knees bent. Place your hands behind your head; fingers can be interlocked or placed on the outer sides at the back of your head. Any hand placement between the two positions mentioned will be acceptable.

The next part of the crunch is to lift your shoulders off the mat, raising your head towards your knees, while supporting your neck without pulling on it.

Doing crunches this way, instead of the old-school way, will reduce chances of injury and give you better/safer results.

That is your basic *Transformation by Design* workout. There are many things you can build on in regard to movement, but this is the foundation. There are many ways to manage yourself so that you are functioning pain-free and at your best self.

You have been working at the routine for a few months now; you are doing 12 minutes of cardio every other day, and the resistance part of the workout at least 3 times per week. To recap the four areas: chest, legs, back and core.

The resistance part of the workout can take as little as 4 minutes. Start by doing 30 seconds for each body part. After each exercise take a 30-second break. After every set, take 1 minute to rest before starting again. Continue to add sets as you improve.

Your goal is to do the 4 exercises 5 times. That whole process should take 30 minutes or less, depending on how long you take your breaks. I recommend taking 30 seconds between each exercise, and 1 minute between rounds. For newbies or anyone just starting back, you can add 30 seconds to the rest period between rounds.

Some of you might decide to do your cardio and resistance training on the same day, and then rest and rejuvenate on your days off. Great decision—whatever works best for you and your schedule.

Start with 12 minutes of interval/cardio. This will help to warm up and loosen your muscles. Now you can start the resistance part of your workout. The whole program can be done in under 30 minutes.

When you get to the point where you can do 5 rounds of resistance training and 12 minutes of interval cardio training, you are at an optimal level of fitness and should be extremely proud of yourself.

When you follow this program. You will have every other day to exercise your mind and your spiritual self.

I find meditation very beneficial for overall health and meditation. I believe it is the bridge between one's mental and spiritual reality.

Some people prefer to do yoga, which is another choice you can do on your days off.

Some of you might decide to read; others may decide to listen to an audio book or some inspiring music. Do whatever you need to do in order to feel better about yourself and others. You might want to go dancing or singing. It doesn't matter what it is, as long as it raises your vibration and keeps you moving.

Have fun, it's your time to enjoy your life the way you want to. When you reach the thirty-day mark of the Transformation by Design program, keep challenging yourself.

At this place in the program, it should be routine. To keep yourself on track, get a journal and keep records of your workouts and activities. Record any and all the good things that you experience each day. Use this record as your blue print in the Transformation by Design journey.

Equipment Type and Use

This chapter is for some of you that might be uncertain about what type of equipment you should use. I put together a list of some of the things that are inexpensive and can be used from the comfort of your home. You can do all the exercises mentioned in this book, with a minimal amount of equipment and space.

I suggest a yoga mat or something you can lay down on comfortably. I also suggest therapeutic bands in different resistances or strengths. Check the colour code system to find the appropriate band strength.

Your physical therapist or trainer would be the best person to recommend the proper band strength. For the people not using a trainer, you can purchase therapeutic bands at most fitness stores and drug stores.

The colour code goes from the lighter colour being the least resistant, to the darker band being more resistant.

Start with a band that you can do 10 repetitions with good form before moving on to a higher resistance band.

The next tool I would like to introduce is the tubing. Tubings are like therapeutic bands except they look like a rubber rope with handles. The handles on the tubings allow for more variety and execution of exercises. They also come in a colour code system similar to the therapeutic bands.

The therapeutic bands and the tubings are two great pieces of equipment for resistance that are efficient and effective for home use. They are also great for traveling. They can fit into your carry-on luggage, so you can keep working out while on vacation.

One of my favourite exercise tools or equipment is the exercise or stability ball. The stability ball comes in a variety of sizes. They are normally measured in centimetres or inches. The sizes range from 45 centimetres to 85 centimetres. The proper fit is determined by the person sitting on the ball with feet flat on the floor, in a 90-degree angle at the knees.

In general, if you are under 5 feet tall, you would use a 45 centimetre ball. A person between 5 feet and 5 feet 10 would use a 55 centimetre ball. Someone between 5' 11" and 6' 5" would use a 65 or 75 centimetre ball.

The best method is to have the person sit on the stability ball and measure the angle they are at. If their hips drop below their knees, then you know the ball is too small. Seeing the hips above the knee line indicates that the ball is too big.

When you have a yoga mat, some therapeutic bands, tubings, dumbbells or free weights, and a stability ball, you have all the equipment you need for a full body workout.

All that's missing is a transformational program and instructions on proper technique. You can find videos on the proper use of the equipment and the techniques, to get the best results possible, on my website.

Go to www.coachty.ca for videos and exercises.

Chapter 8

Mind Your Own Business

When I say "mind your own business," I'm talking about focusing your mind on the business of you. Take care of yourself the way you would take care of a successful business. Start by putting together a plan of action, in as much detail as possible. Take a survey or scrutinize yourself in every area. For example: 1) What time did you wake up? 2) What was the first thing you did upon waking (i.e. brush teeth, shower, use the toilet, etc.)?

3) Did you check your phone, or turn on the radio or TV? 4) Did you have breakfast and if so, what did you have? 5) Did you get dressed before or after breakfast? 6) Did you read the newspaper? 7) Did you have to help someone else in the morning, like your children, etc.? 8) Record all of your activities, and everything that goes into your mouth (i.e. water, coffee, food, cigarettes, gum, and everything and anything).

Continue recording your activities during the day. Keep this up until you are back in bed, where you started. The next step is to take the recorded information and consider how you might make healthier choices the next day.

When you have completed this one major task, you will be halfway to designing your transformation.

The next big step is to clean your surroundings, as your life will be healthier and happier. You should start cleaning any messes that have a negative effect on you. Get rid of some of your old clothing and things you haven't used in a while. Look for places where there's lots of clutter, and tidy them up.

Your fridge and your cupboards should be cleaned out. Record everything so that you have a place to start and a plan. You should replace what is old and unhealthy, with good nutritious food. Look for a good water filter, and use it on a regular basis so that you stay hydrated.

Make a commitment to complete the task at hand. Let someone close to you know what you intend to do, and then go and do it. Go back to the beginning of the book and start doing the breathing exercises if you haven't done them yet.

Now you have a record of what you were doing. Take some time to think about what you want and the life you would like to live. Keep a journal so that you can go back and see all of the habits you changed along your transformation journey.

Keeping your mind active, focused, and positive takes discipline. That being the case, how do you improve your discipline? I say, one day at a time. Start with the small things and then add on new things that you want to discipline yourself to do.

For example, while brushing your teeth in the morning, you might want to start doing some light easy stretches.

When you continue to do the stretches for 21 days, it becomes a habit, and soon it will be like brushing your teeth. You have the power to add on to your basic habits any time you like and you can keep building more positive habits over time.

I know it sounds easier than it will be to do, but how much do you want to transform your life and become the best version of you there is?

To make the changes, you have to put in the work. No one can do it for you. Action is where the rubber hits the road in manifesting and creating the things you want for yourself. I suggest you start doing something that will bring you closer to your goals, right away, with no delay.

We are living in a time where you can learn just about anything from YouTube or on the internet. Take advantage of the time we are living in. Imagine going back 30–40 years. Think about it for a minute. There were no cell phones, so it wasn't easy to get in contact with people. Most people wrote letters as a form of communication. No one writes letters anymore. How about GPS? When I was working as a district manager for Dickie Dee Ice Cream, I would have to use a map and plan my day the night before, so that I would have a better idea of where I had to go and how long it would take.

Most of the population born in the 90s and after have no clue how to use a map or how to write a letter. We as boomers have that old-school training and discipline, so let's start using it again.

When we combine what we know with the new technology of today, we can do wonders and achieve whatever we want.

I want you to be fit, healthy, and pain-free, but I can't do it for you. All I can do is show you what I do, and how it has helped me throughout the years. Over my 35 years in the fitness industry, I have seen many transformations, so I know it is possible to change and be the best version of yourself. Start paying it forward, and you will see some amazing results.

You are your business. Like I said at the beginning of the chapter, *mind your own business*. I am talking about being conscious of what's happening with you. Take inventory, record all of the areas in your life that you are dissatisfied with, and then start working on them one at a time.

I came across a book called *The Self-Care Solution*, by Jennifer Ashton. I liked the way she transformed her life by changing one aspect of it at a time. Every month, she would take on a challenge; by the end of the year, 12 new habits were formed.

Below, I have listed her chapters and the habits that she changed to transform her life:

January: Dry month. This is for anyone that drinks alcohol on a social basis.

February: Push-ups and Planks. Start with 25 push-ups and a 30-second plank; increase weekly for the month.

March: Meditation. Starting your day about 20–30 minutes earlier would be beneficial. There are guided meditation audio programs and books available.

April: Cardio. Follow the transformation program. Start with 1–2 minutes of cardio at a normal rate, and increase it to a more intense rate every 30 seconds, intermittent training.

May: Less meat and more plants. This is a great way to help lose weight and eat healthier.

Hydration: You can follow the transformation method and use some of the suggestions in the book.

July: More steps. Get out and get moving more, or you can do the transformation routine.

August: Start by doing 30 minutes phone-free, every day for 30 days. Then add the television for the same amount of time.

September: Sugarless. Check your labels to see the sugar content in the food you are eating; keep the amount below 25 grams.

October: Stretching. Focus on stretching, or do some yoga or qigong to keep your body limber.

November: Sleep. This is the time to regenerate and rejuvenate. Studies show that getting 8 hours of sleep will help you function at an optimal level.

Laughter: Focus on things that make you feel good and raise your vibration. Go to a comedy club, watch some funny movies, or listen to a comedian.

Chapter 9

Designing Your Transformation

How do you create your transformation? The best way is to start with your breathing technique. Practise some deep breathing exercises, which will help clean out some toxins in your body and open your mind to bigger things.

Next, focus on what you are putting in your mouth and record what you are eating in a journal. Then make appropriate substitutions for the junk foods, with healthy nutrition based foods.

Follow up by making sure you are hydrated. When these first steps become habits, then you need to start moving more and exercising on a regular basis.

The Transformation by Design program gives you the guidelines you need in order to design your own program. Just play with the numbers and do what works best for you.

I have tried many types of alternative therapies to help improve my functioning abilities and to alleviate pain.

One of the best things I have found is the use of qigong. I prefer qigong to other martial arts or energy moving techniques. I find it easier to learn than tai chi, even though it's very similar.

Tai chi is the foundation for many of the martial arts, especially kung fu. I have studied martial arts for many years. I started studying karate and kickboxing, and then kung fu, which I found very intriguing.

I recognized that most of the kung fu styles came from tai chi. On my quest to further my knowledge, I came across qigong as a way to direct the internal energy and help heal and improve my overall health.

Qigong is a method of unblocking energy channels, so that you can improve your health by allowing full energy flow. This works on the same premise as acupuncture and acupressure. With acupuncture, you're using needles to direct your energy flow, and it opens the meridians so that your energy is not prohibited. In acupressure, you are just using pressure points on certain areas of your body to allow the qi or energy to flow.

Qigong uses movement like tai chi. The movements are always flowing like water. This flowing movement allows the qi or energy to revitalize your body and improve your health.

When the Chi or Qi is flowing, you unblock the meridians, which corrects and helps the energy flow through your body. I find it easy to learn and easy to do. I study and practice modern qigong as a way to improve my energy level and my overall health.

Meditation is another great way to raise your energy and vibration while helping you breathe and focus better. Meditation is basically just calming your mind and focusing on your breathing. You should start by doing 5 minutes at a time until you can get to 10 minutes without drifting. See if you can get to half an hour. The more you do it, the more benefits you will receive, and the better you will feel.

Meditation is best performed in a quiet place in a seated position or a yoga position. I love to incorporate another alternative therapy using essential oils. Studying the use of essential oils has been educational and beneficial to me. When you incorporate meditation with essential oils, wonderful things happen. Your mind clears, your focus improves, and your energy and vibrational levels rise.

I have mentioned several alternative therapies and healing methods, and have a few more to share. Reiki is another source of energy therapy that has worked wonders for some. I have experienced and studied the benefits of Reiki myself, and I recommend it to my clients.

Looking back at all the alternative methods and techniques, you realize that they are all related to increasing your vibration and energy levels. The use of crystals is also an energy and vibrational enhancer.

In the Transformation by Design studio, you will find a combination of many of these vibrational and energy enhancing methods. I also like to incorporate modern technology by using affirmations, and subliminal and other mind-enhancing techniques.

In my research and studies, I have come across other technologies. One that I tried and find very interesting is Voxx socks. They have a technology that is built into socks and inserts in your shoes. This technology is new, different and exciting. I have experienced some of the demonstrations and I find them beneficial especially when it comes to balance and pain relief.

One thing I do on a continuous basis is research and look for new and promising products and techniques that will help me and my clients.

Ho'oponopono is another technique that interests me. Ho'oponopono is a Hawaiian mental cleansing technique that was modernized by Morrnah Simeona. She shared this modern version of Ho'oponopono throughout the United States, Asia, and Europe.

Morrnah was a practitioner of lomilomi massage and, for 10 years, she owned and operated health spas at Kahala Hilton and Royal Hawaiian hotels.

At these spas, she would combine her healing form of Ho'oponopono for a vast array of clients, many of which were celebrities, like Lyndon B. Johnson, Jackie Kennedy, and Arnold Palmer.

Modern Ho'oponopono One Step Further

Dr. Ihaleakala Hew Len, a student who worked closely with Morrnah, is probably best known for curing criminally insane patients in Hawaii, without ever seeing any of them.

In 2005, Dr. Joe Vitale wrote an article about Dr. Hew Len. Since then, they have come together to conduct seminars and teach classes to people who are interested in becoming certified Ho'oponopono practitioners.

I have taken the program and I find it very interesting and beneficial. I recommend this program to anyone looking to transform and improve their life.

*The information about Ho'oponopono was taken from Joe Vitale's basic Ho'oponopono Practitioner Certification course.

At this point, I have shared many of the techniques and alternative therapies that I believe change lives. If you have been following along and doing the exercises and suggestions, then give yourself a big hooray! You earned it.

Now the focus should be on your mind and emotions. This is the next level of vibration and a major part in your overall wellness and health.

Keep your mind sharp and active by doing mind stimulating exercises. Some examples are reading, watching trivia and mystery shows, taking personal development courses, etc.

Learning new skills is a great way to stimulate your mind and raise your vibration. Playing an instrument or singing are some fun mind activities. Some prefer doing more physical things like playing chess, darts, pool, and/or some organized team sport.

One of the things I enjoy is Djembe drumming or hand drumming. I love the vibration and rhythm the instrument makes. It's a great tool for stress management, mind stimulation, and body movement. Djembe drumming helps me increase my vibrational level and enhances my overall health.

You can drum on your own or in a group. The benefits are amazing.

First, you are using your physical body to beat the drums, which in turns helps you burn calories; and second, you increase your hand/ear development. Before you know it, you will be playing along to popular songs.

To recap, by playing the drums, you will be getting exercise, learning a new instrument, managing your stress level, stimulating your mind, and elevating your vibration.

This is a great way to feel and be. When you are at that frequency and vibrational level, your energy will be at its best, and you will be at your best.

Chapter 10

Create Your Challenge

I enjoy challenging myself and mastering that challenge. For me, that old-school determination kicks in and I am totally engaged.

I decided to do a personal challenge while writing this book.

The challenge involved doing 100 push-ups a day for 30 days. I started on July 25, 2019.

I completed the challenge on August 25, 2019. This is how it went down. When I started, I decided to weigh myself and take the basic measurements, which consisted of chest, waist, hips, and arms. At that time, I wanted to lose a few pounds and put on some muscle. I got started by doing 25 push-ups straight.

I took a rest and did another 25 push-ups about 20 minutes later. I completed two more sets of 25 push-ups. The thing I liked about the challenge of doing 100 push-ups in a day was that I didn't have to do them all at the same time.

By my fourth day I was doing 50 push-ups straight the first thing in the morning, and then 50 push-ups about 1 hour later. When I got to the last third of the challenge, I would do 60 or 70 push-ups straight and then complete the remainder about 20 minutes to an hour later.

On my last day of the challenge, I did 80 push-ups straight, and then completed the 20 push-ups a few minutes later. I completed 3000 push-ups in 30 days and it felt very satisfying. I could then show my clients and readers that when you put your mind to something, you can do it. I also increased my muscle mass and reduced my weight by 7 or 8 pounds. These two things were the added benefits of setting a goal and sticking to it.

When it was finished, I wanted to do something more. I decided to challenge myself while improving my body's strength and overall wellness. Since I had been doing push-ups for 30 days and my body was responding well to the new routine, I thought it would be great to do a different body part. I decided to focus on my lower body as it is an essential part of balance and core strength.

Legs would be the body part, and squats would be the exercise.
For all of you eager active agers, if you feel like a challenge, join me.

This squat challenge will be conducted the same way the push-up challenge was done.

Start by doing 100 squats per day for 30 days. For anyone that is recovering from an injury or are a novice, you can modify the number. Make sure it is enough to challenge yourself. Remember it is 100 squats per day and they don't have to be completed at one time.

For anyone that finds exercise difficult but can physically do at least 1 push-up and 1 squat, then challenge yourself to do 25 per day for 30 days. Some of you might decide that 50 is a good place to start. Whatever you do, stick to it and complete the 30 days.

You will be very happy when you complete the challenge. You will be rewarded with discipline, tenacity, a stronger body and improved balance. Plus you might lose some body fat and/or inches. Now you can keep things going and form a new habit. Soon that habit becomes a lifestyle. This is how you design your transformation, one challenge at a time.

When you have completed one challenge, it will be time to start a new one. When you get that feeling of accomplishment, you will want to experience it again. This time you could do two things that support each other. For example, doing the push-up challenge and hydration challenge. Find the area you want to transform the most and challenge yourself for 30 days, but do it a day at a time. Be proud of yourself at the end of the day, knowing you did what you committed to do.

One thing you should do is have a calendar that you can write on. Every day, cross off the task when you finish it. When you need a little motivation, just take a look and see how far you have come.

When your health has improved and you feel fit and your weight is where you want it to be, you can focus on other areas of your life that you want to transform. Perhaps you want to increase your knowledge by reading more books. Let's say you want to read 3 books in 30 days, or whatever number you can handle. Commit to your goal and do it like you did the other challenges.

Another example might be relationships. The person looking to get into a relationship needs to be around other people. One way to get around others with similar interests is to take some classes or get involved in some community work where you are helping others. Take a dance class or try a meetup group. There are meetup groups for everything you can think of like photography, social dancing, or exercise. The list goes on and on. Take the time to investigate the many opportunities out there. You just might find the right person and learn a new skill at the same time.

For someone already in a relationship, one of the greatest gifts is appreciation for your partner. Make it a challenge: Every day you have to give your partner a compliment that will make them feel better about themselves.

The first compliment should be in the morning, the second compliment in the afternoon, and the third one just before going to bed. Make sure you do at least one compliment a day to start.

Try the challenge above for just 3 days. If you like the results continue for the week and before you know it, 30 days have gone by. How about your relationship? Is it totally awesome or at least a lot better than it was?

For anyone that completes this challenge, please let me hear the details of your story.
Send to: coachmedpro@gmail.com

After attempting a third push-up challenge in March and completing it in April. I wanted to do something different, since we are in an uncertain time, with the covid 19 pandemic.

The practice of social distancing is in effect. I started doing my exercise classes via Zoom. This allows me to work with my clients and keep the connection as well. I thought it would be a great time to create a new challenge. This new challenge would be slightly different.

The challenge is to do a plank for 30 seconds then increase the holding time of the plank by thirty seconds each week. I have a small group of about 6-8 people participating in this challenge with me.

The first week of the challenge all participants will do a plank for one minute. The second week the plank time will be increased to one minute and thirty seconds. The third week a two minute plank. The final week we will perform a three minute plank.

The above examples are just a few ways to show how you can transform yourself by creating challenges. The type of challenge you decide to choose is up to you. I want to coach you on how to use them to get what you want. The challenge is to design a program that will transform you to your best self.

I wish for you to take on a challenge every 30 days. The choice is yours on which challenge you want to undertake; just make sure it is something that will raise your vibration and your energy.
Keep an open mind and be flexible with the way you think and the

alternatives you choose.

Anyone living in Canada or anyplace where cannabis is legal, should do their research and see if CBD is something they might want to try. The non-psychoactive chemical in the plant that helps with seizures and relieves pain without having any side effects.

With the many ways of using CBD, you might find it a beneficial way to relieve your pain.

Keep on searching and researching alternative methods and techniques to improve health and relieve pain. There is relief at all levels, including the physical level, the mental level and the spiritual level. You may need it on many levels.

Identify the problem, do some self-examination, and follow some of the techniques in this book. I know there will be some ailments and issues that you won't be able to determine on your own. A medical professional can help in this case, but don't just agree with whatever diagnosis they come up with. Get a second opinion, especially if it is something serious like an operation or some life changing event.

Always be conscious of your body. Like I always tell my clients, no one knows you like you do. You know what you are capable of doing, and you have the power to do it.

Most people give their power to someone else because of a title that person holds. If you are connected holistically—body, mind and spirit—you will find the answers you need in order to be your best self and live a pain-free active life.

Chapter 11

In Conclusion

I have shared my story with each of you and you are aware of some of the challenges I have had to overcome. You now know some of the methods and alternative therapies I used to continually enhance and improve myself. I hope you will start to use as many of these alternative therapies as you can, to help you be the best version of you.

You have dedicated your time, effort and energy to reading this book, and I hope you have been using the techniques. Now that you are feeling better and you want to do more things to keep your energy level high, it's time to try something new. Get out of your comfort zone. If you are a boomer, then you are in the last third or quarter of your life. Did you do all the things you wanted to do, travelled to places you wanted to go, learned skills you wanted to learn?

Like I said at the beginning, if you are breathing, then you have a chance to improve your life and do all of the things you've wanted to do.

Use all the tools you have to live the life you want. When you are happy with yourself and things are the way you want them to be, you can focus your energy on helping others and building positive healthy relationships.

When your vibration and energy levels are high, you will want to share the experience with family and friends. How about sharing it with your children and/or grandchildren? Now, take a bigger step and share it with strangers at a school, nursing home or day care.

Sharing the skills you learned from this book is a great way to help the whole planet. When you help someone their vibration level is increased. The two of you, and anyone else you share the information with, will create a *synergy* or combined higher vibration, which in turn will affect everyone it touches. It becomes contagious—the good feeling, the higher energy and a more positive outlook.

That is my dream, to see all creatures on planet earth living in harmony. Everything counts, so do your part and transform your place on earth.

Now take that nice deep rejuvenating breath, and with an open mind, envision what you want and the kind of life you want to live. Get out and have some fun.

Now you have the knowledge and techniques to be a mentor and help someone transform their life by design.

Pay it forward. This may be a life changer for someone else and the greatest part is that it will help you increase your vibration and your frequency.
The waiting game is over. We are in the last stretch, so give it all you

In Conclusion

got. The journey of life ends like it started—with a simple breath.

With that breath say the cleansing words of the "Ho'oponopono" technique.

I'm sorry - Please forgive me - Thank you - I Love you

www.ingramcontent.com/pod-product-compliance
Lightning Source LLC
Chambersburg PA
CBHW060414090426
42734CB00011B/2311